Bug in a rug

Russell Punter

Illustrated by David Semple

"I need my sleep tonight,"
says Bug.

"Tomorrow I start work for Slug."

Bug glugs hot
chocolate from
a mug.

Then snuggles
up inside
his rug.

Bug hugs his bear.
He starts to nap.

Then he hears barking...

Loud party music
shakes the wall.

Below, a baby starts to bawl.

Bug plugs his ears,

but all too soon...

Owl is hooting
at the moon.

T-wit t-woo!

A car alarm adds to the row.

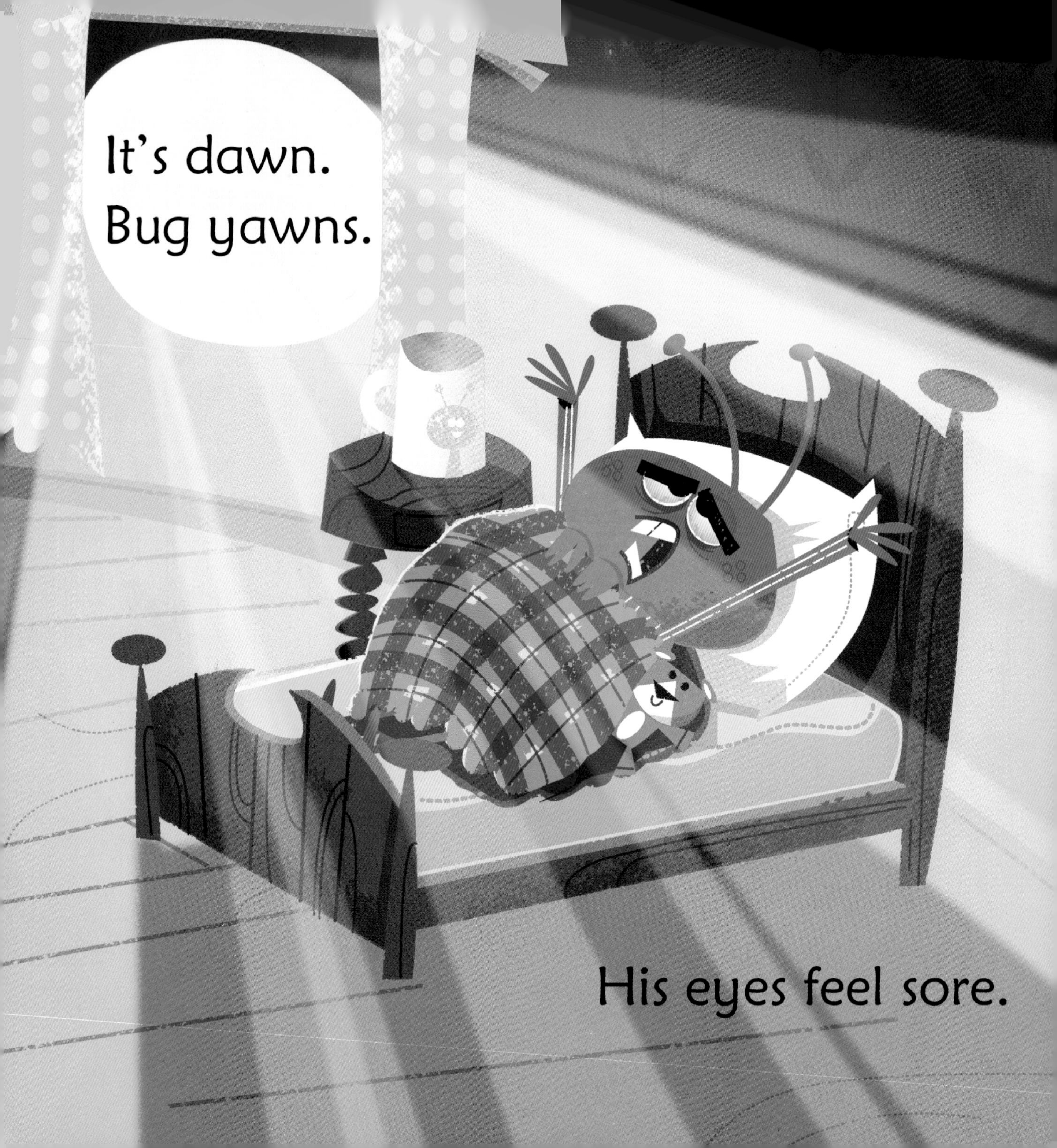

It's dawn.
Bug yawns.

His eyes feel sore.

He plods to work at Slug's Rug Store.

"Quick march," shouts
Slug. "Don't stand about."

"I feel so sleepy now," thinks Bug.

"And all these rugs look soft and snug..."

When Slug comes back
at ten o'clock...

Slug's Rug Store

...his store is packed. It's quite a shock.

About phonics

Phonics is a method of teaching reading used extensively in today's schools. At its heart is an emphasis on identifying the *sounds* of letters, or combinations of letters, that are then put together to make words. These sounds are known as phonemes.

Starting to read

Learning to read is an important milestone for any child. The process can begin well before children start to learn letters and put them together to read words. The sooner children can discover books and enjoy stories and language, the better they will be prepared for reading themselves, first with the help of an adult and then independently.

You can find out more about phonics on the Usborne Very First Reading website, **www.usborne.com/veryfirstreading** (US readers go to **www.veryfirstreading.com**). Click on the **Parents** tab at the top of the page, then scroll down and click on **About synthetic phonics**.

Phonemic awareness

An important early stage in pre-reading and early reading is developing phonemic awareness: that is, listening out for the sounds within words. Rhymes, rhyming stories and alliteration are excellent ways of encouraging phonemic awareness.

In this story, your child will soon identify the *u* sound, as in **bug** and **rug**. Look out, too, for rhymes such as **wall** – **bawl** and **nap** – **yap**.

Hearing your child read

If your child is reading a story to you, don't rush to correct mistakes, but be ready to prompt or guide if he or she is struggling. Above all, do give plenty of praise and encouragement.

Edited by Jenny Tyler and Lesley Sims
Designed by Sam Whibley

Reading consultants: Alison Kelly and Anne Washtell

First published in 2015 by Usborne Publishing Ltd., Usborne House, 83-85 Saffron Hill, London EC1N 8RT, England.
www.usborne.com Copyright © 2015 Usborne Publishing Ltd.